Casey Bailey is a writer, performer and educator, born and raised in Nechells, Birmingham, UK. C--- Poet Laureate 2020 - 2022.

Casey was named as one o'
'30 under 30' of 2018. Casey
he was made a Fellow of the
named the Greater Birmingha   .. .. and Culture
2020.

Casey released his debut full collection of poetry, *Adjusted* in 2018 with Verve Poetry Press. His debut play 'GrimeBoy' was commissioned by the Birmingham Rep in 2020. Casey's poetry has featured in a number of anthologies and he was commissioned by the BBC to write 'The Ballad of The Peaky Blinders' in 2019. In 2020 the poem was internationally recognised, winning a Webby Award. Casey has performed his poetry nationally, and internationally. *Please Do Not Touch* is his second full collection.

Raymond Antrobus said of Casey:

'With Casey, we get to meet a story-teller as well as a poet, who is honing a kind of cinematic and musical language. I am so happy to see voices like his emerging from Birmingham.'

Please Do Not Touch

Casey Bailey

Burning Eye

BurningEyeBooks
Never Knowingly
Mainstream

This edition published by Burning Eye Books 2021

www.burningeye.co.uk

@burningeyebooks

Burning Eye Books
15 West Hill, Portishead, BS20 6LG

ISBN 978-1-913958-05-3

PLEASE DO NOT TOUCH

For Leon.
We can't be with you anymore, but you will always be with us.

I've seen some turn their ideas
into their identity
and cling to it for years.

I've seen others use kindness.

Leon Priestnall

CONTENTS

WAKING

There is a violence to her tossing and turning
that speaks to an ingrained experience of barbarity.
Her eyes-shut-tight whimper relays echoes
of the gunshots thundering through her mind.

Burst berries sprayed across his jumper
like they used to when she fed him at
that high chair. On this day, his jumper
will be cast aside by paramedics.

She is fired from the barrel of her bed too quick
to feel the damp of a soaked pillowcase;
she is racing to a room, searching for a boy
who isn't there. He's never been there;

she moved to this house to escape his ghost,
to save his brother, to sleep until morning.

LAST

He always loved to have the last
word. Wasn't like he never listened, just
he always made sure you did too.

Today the squint of your eyes is audible,
wet. He can feel the downpour
of your goodbye landing on his skin.

He is choking on blood, or apologies,
the struggle to verbalise his demons,
the struggle to live beyond the now.

He is struggling, but he manages to
force out a word –

bro.

How do you calm a soul as it leaves?
How do you cling to a life already lost?
He always loved to have the last word.

Last breath like a floorboard creaking,
creeping through trachea, reaching
the sleeping, waking their astral bodies.

19.02.20

There's no rain without flowers, you said
Blundering through affirmations
They press scalpel through torso
No flowers without rain
We laugh at mistakes
Embracing how
Magical
He is
Born

Born
He is
Magical
Embracing how
We laugh at mistakes
No flowers without rain
They press scalpel through torso
Blundering through affirmations
There's no rain without flowers, you said

ANGELA DAVIS SAID MORE #1

Susie King Taylor was a nurse and a teacher
                                    In
persistent efforts to educate herself during slavery
                                                        Susie
                            ran great risks

                            compelled to

acquire   knowledge   to share it with their people

            that post emancipation phenomenon

            a yearning born of centuries of denial
                                    Women on the edge of
                                                Scripture
                    Painfully

                            organized

            To assist their Black sisters   determined to
wipe out illiteracy

HEAVY. ALWAYS.

Running like children.
Water, whispering like traffic
through double glazing.

From the bench
at Kedleston Hall
I hear grass crushed
beneath city-calloused feet.

Spine, curved
by concrete slabs,
unravels in the presence
of lifeless leaves,

and still
        even now
when I can't hear the city
I know it isn't silent.

Blissful ignorance is a fallacy;
the owners of land and life
who inhabited this hall
were never unaware;

the burden of care
is carried by slaves
how I carry the sound
of the city. Heavy. Always.

SAME

The solid stone pillars are made from resin,
their guts hollow, like yesterday's bottle,
hanging heavy as today's hangover.

Power's not a body; it's an outfit.

Scagliola is wearing marble's face.
If you knew neither, you'd swear them twins.
If it fits where it sits, who'd ask questions?

Nothing more precious than perception.

He pilfers without pause. Men on your ship,
blade to ribs, prizes prised from the perished.
Voyager, captain, explorer, hero.

Judgement based on standing, more than standards.

ENERGY

The Gs on his Gucci bag don't look right,
inside as empty as cold gun barrels.
Still, the weight of the threat reverberates.

Power's not a body; it's an outfit.

Cubic zirconia look like diamonds.
Only light penetrates this fallacy.
Eyes see before looking, trust what they know.

Nothing more precious than perception.

He takes without nuance, hand in pocket,
smile on face, your life or your possessions.
Hooligan, crook, thug, criminal, villain.

Judgement based on standing, more than standards.

EVERY BOY WHO DIES IN THE GHETTO IS ME

Maybe I was too young.
They say your life flashes
before your eyes. Maybe
I haven't seen enough life;
the only light I saw came
with a bang attached.
The only thing I saw was death,
grinning like a schoolboy
who takes money at lunch
time, snatching before
speaking, without care.

There wasn't rain on
the day I fell. The street
could not clean itself.
A woman who looks like
my mother had to clean
the blood; she saw her
son turn from smiles
to spray, from stains to suds,
to silence. She saw her
boy, barely born, buried
before she saw him live.

CURFEW BREAKERS

THERE IS A LESSON   so
      basic   the details are

      enforcing a curfew

          The policemen
    shoot curfew breakers

        that is clearly illegal.

            a warning

that stabs the eye   if the eye is not
        obtuse or corrupt.
    This lesson

called upon to intercept and destroy

      It simply will not happen.

      we will make it technically impossible

         The mission   sabotaged.

      long enough to make the whole operation impossible
              at   last

31.08.05

'You can't just pray to me now.'
God's voice, in my head, is cold.
I am cold. There is a hole in my
back that wasn't there this morning.
I am here and there simultaneously;
I am feet on the floor and blood
on the blade. I am cold. I feel cold.

There is a hole in my back

'We had one die the other week.'
The paramedic talking out of the ceiling
light tells tales of the man who dropped
dead on arrival. Says his body must've
thought he had made it to safety. I try
to remember to focus on staying alive.

Focus on staying alive

'She wouldn't say that if you were dying.'
My voice, this time. Rationalising my own
mortality is a delicate thread to cling to,
but what do you do? Let go? Lean into
rapid pulse; blink for just a moment too long.

Rationalising my own mortality

WHEN THE ROLL IS CALLED UP YONDER

If tears were dirt, we would have filled this hole before we placed you in it. We shovel, now, and I promise myself the same thing I did the last time I stood on the edge of a grave, on the edge of a breakdown: *My only friend will be rage now*. I have buried too many friends to trust in their permanence; I can only have faith that rage will return again and again. Today I am burning, the anger inside is piping and indiscriminate. I'm mad at your dad, the man who failed to show up so many times but stands here like your funeral can serve as his redemption; I feel the seed of fury taking root in my stomach as I look to the boys who took today for a fashion parade and stand far back on the path now, terrified of mud on their Pradas. I am boiling, because I told you not to go there, told you it wasn't safe, you wouldn't listen, you never listened. I always loved that about you, the 'I told you so' moments that we shared are my favourites, and neither one was always right but we always got to talk about it. Not this time. This time I put my arm around your mother, as we fill a grave with tears, and memories and hopes for a future that nobody needs anymore; our dreams for you are VHS tapes now, still holding stories, never to be told. All we have now is dirt, dropping on wood, scratching like your spirit on the inside, like our spirit on the outside, all we have left now is earth, crumbling beneath our feet. Our eyes check the clouds, see if they will break for you. We sing graveside hymns, hoping our harmonies will open heaven for you to return there; even those who don't believe sing like they do. They do this for your grandmother and her church friends, they know that she has lost more than she should already. They will not steal her faith, today.

LIBRARY

This room is book lovers,
is a testament,
is two generations.
This room is additional shelf space.

This room where children read
politics by the fireplace.
These politics that placed
children by fires. This room

coated, now, in dust or ash.
We discover how weeds
became flowers, how light
became control. Controlled.

This room is a doorway.
This room is a boundary.
This room is a foundation.
This room knows no ceiling.

GATEHOUSE

I am council housing and council pop,
If you're not full, drink more water.
The sound of Saturday soup bubbling,
Meat seasoned since yesterday.
Hardo bread sliced thicker than grief
You know say it's 'hard dough', right?
Where he who can't hear must feel.
You tink say me and you is size?

I walk through life with bricks in my bag.
Sometimes what's heavy is inside.
I step on the path to the biggest house.
Starve not to rob, before you rob not to starve.
'Gatehouse' bigger than childhood home.
More than you need is always greed.
I know my mother would smile now,
Walk with confidence wherever you go.
Knowing they would frown if they saw me.
How they feel is their business.

TROMPE-L'OEIL

The Black boy with the metal collar
is a 'page boy' chained like the horse
he holds. A black beauty, a beast
braced by the man he serves.

Out of frame there is champagne
pissing from the heavens –
intoxicating. The statue lions
have been roaring into the vacuum,

animated in protestation,
and here, in this corridor
between actuality and invention –

the Black boy
in the collar is
a page boy.

SOUP

Today, you ate tomato soup like it was the first meal that you had eaten in days. You had half a cheese sandwich for lunch, at one thirty. There is soup on the table and bread in your hair, you look like Mowgli from The Jungle Book, if Mowgli had eaten soup, and you smile as the yoghurt is placed in front of you. You look at yoghurt how I looked at your mother the day I met her, how I looked at your mother at four o'clock this morning, as she sighed in her sleep, dreaming of you and your ways. You look at yoghurt how I looked at your mother when I found her in the art room, painting, at college. Her paintbrush darting like sparrows on autumn mornings, leaving crimsons and caramels in their wake. I knew then that she would spend her life both being and making beauty. She feeds you yoghurt. I take the wipes out. There is soup all over the floor.

ANGELA DAVIS SAID MORE #2

a working-class suffrage movement was

a mass demonstration
to be observed all over the world as

its   leaders and activists

and, in fact

there could never be

socialism

While   the Socialist party

did not acknowledge the unique
oppression of Black people.   Black people

required   defense
of their rights to be equal and free as a group

SUSPENDED

The light in the hospital toilet flickers, the fragile beat of
a heart during surgery. We remind each other how
strong you are, trying to siphon that strength to
restrain the furious estuaries of our eyelids.
I switch tactics, from rapid blinking to
calm, solid eye contact, knowing
that showing my weaknesses
would be accepting yours;
I can't betray you. The
word hanging in the
air stinks of blood,
tastes of death.
They'll tell us
that you're
gone.
They never
say dead. It
doesn't change
the fact, it will not
change the bulb in the
light, it just flickers until it
can't. We stand in darkness,
telling each other that you have
travelled to the luminescence that you
deserve. At your funeral, I'll hold my sister
in my arms, let the tsunami break my eyelids like you
broke my faith. There's no strength in denial now. They'll
tell me time will heal. I know now that we all run out of time.

THE OLD MAN

The old man has seen things
that we haven't; his scruffy coat
doesn't do his grandeur justice.
Old and knobbled, I'd imagine he hobbled here.

Weighed down and wearied
by the knowledge that so many
who were born beneath him
are gone now, those who provided shade
at his birth are barely even memories.

He is not the last man standing,
but what is company when your past
is the longest and your future
is the strongest? Who do you sit with
at lunch time when you have eaten
the ancestors of your peers and written
recipes for their unborn children?

He is not old like your bedbound nana.
He is old like royal palaces, surrounded
by tower blocks who have youth
but little more. There is no point in learning
his story to share his legacy.
When you are gone, he will tell it
for himself. You will not feature.

The old man has seen things
that we haven't. He will see things
that we will not.

I THOUGHT I HEARD

Must've been the way the bottle top
connected with the concrete,
must've been the way roses
settled upon coffin tops,
must've been the way tears
pierced the soil beneath us,
must've been the way my homie
collided with the pavement.

Perhaps it was my son's flinch,
my hope that bottle tops would
always scare him to his core,
let him be sure
that just because monsters
don't live under his bed,
that doesn't mean
they don't exist.

I thought I heard a shot.
Whether there was one or not,
I heard it, didn't miss a single stride,
just sighed. You cannot kill
what is dead with noise.

WATER WORKS

The fountain at Witley Court
won't speak to us today.
He who shouts sits silent for once.

You say, 'Maybe it's been running
off slave tears this whole time.
Maybe it's finally dried up?'

IF I SPEAK

Hard to smell the flowers
without inhaling the blood

> *It's OK to appreciate the view*
> *and still see the trauma, you know*

Restraint is the only
resistance I have left

> *You're punishing yourself, hoping*
> *they will feel your pain*

It's not my pain; I only
feel it. I owe them that much

> *Their greatest trick is to make us*
> *feel that our joy is betrayal*

FAMILIAR

It could be from school;
you don't remember every face
and name from those days.

Maybe this boy, who you
know from somewhere,
was in the year above.

When your eyes meet, his
name will rush to the tip
of your tongue and dissipate

into the ether between
here and there. His grimace
will remind you of scraped

knees from your BMX days.
The thunderstorm in your thorax
will break into a frantic scream.

As his eyes close, you travel
into a void of shadows;
you will remember. Too late.

ANGELA DAVIS SAID MORE #3

Of course, the
                    open and public violence
          of racism

                                   often portrayed Black women
as promiscuous and immoral.

                    the simple
          imposition of this attitude

     has always drawn strength from

                    sexual
          conduct towards

                                        their
sisters of color.
                         racism
                    drummed
into   heads   that

they were   an inferior race

     the unwritten policy.

VICEROY

There is a man in my house who I didn't invite.
He eats my food, no permission, no apology;
he beats my children until they bleed, they bawl for me.
I cry for their loss and mine; we're homeless at home.

We celebrate his majesty whilst he is present,
breathe the perfume of his flesh, fragrance of rose and rot.
When his back is turned salt water pours, washing the shores
of our eyeballs. This tide will never turn; we're stranded.

With our land handed to this outlandish outlander,
we now sit uneasy, like the Kohinoor diamond
in a British crown; we will never shine like we did.
There is no light to detain or return in darkness.

Lights out, no sleep, no rest, we weep; he remains, shameless.
There's a man in the house that we used to call home.

TWO SWINGS

And they will not hold hands;
instead they will let little fingers
hang, intertwined. In this bond
they will keep the time he said,
I dunno, man, you're special,
and the time she said, Yeah,
maybe not all boys, just most.
Between this finger link
and his black Air Max 95s
brushing along the side
of her white Air Force 1s
they will hold a phenomenon
that breaks every rule of this
place. They will wrap it warmly
in black tracksuits, dip it in honey,
coat it with Demerara sugar
and rock it, back and forward,
on these swings, under midnight sky.

SWEAR DOWN

I didn't even wanna do it, I had to
will be the final line of his story

Swear down

The chorus from the boys is no
challenge to a liar of his skill

Mom's life

They will not judge him, these words
hold as much weight as his stories

Mad

NO ROD SPARED

When you pause, to wipe the sweat
from your brow, your son will inhale
the ocean and release *sorry* on its waves.
When the tide washes over you
you will hold for a moment. As his wince breaks,
cheeks fall and the tension leaves his shoulders,
you will strike with more potency. Blood
will run from the fault lines across a forearm,
thrown in defence. He will look from behind
this shield for the hatred that he knows must live
in your eyes. His gaze will fall on fear
and trepidation. You walk him to this depth,
let his lungs hold water only to keep him
from drowning at the hands of another.

WHAT THE MOBILE PHONE CAMERAS NEVER CAPTURE

How fear stinks
How grief lands
How death—

THE RUIN

The monument in the garden isn't falling down.
It was built like that; the architect admired
the aesthetic of ancient Athens, dilapidated
statues, leaning like old men on canes
before hip replacements.

Struggle and pain are so romantic and sexy
to those who have never known them.
In a world where the Rottweilers gnaw
their own tails off to wag their stumps
for sympathy, and rhinoceroses shed
their horns for attention, the ruin fits.

With the sunlight splintering off the river,
giving light back to a structure that only throws shade,
and dragonflies jiving across its dance floor,
it is wondrous and elegant and magical
and I wish I never knew its story.

DAYS LIKE THIS

Like water down the drainpipe,
he will spill into the hoodie;
he will settle in the black Air Max 90s
that he keeps for days like this.
Ten toes extending through the sole.
On days like this he could snatch
the stars from the sky and you would
thank him for allowing you to live
to see the darkness. He only knows how
to die and kill, rinse and repeat.
He only knows days like this come every day.
Grim Reaper hoodie and black Air Max
90s, he stays ready for days like this.

WHEN YOUR BROTHER DIED

You spent his fortune on your dreams, built your grand
estate on the back of his stolen wealth like
it was yours – like it was his. He'd have loved it.

Grecian taste, oriental magnificence,
how to dress opportunistic betrayal
so that it may strut. How graceful can greed be?

Who taught you to take so well, which marauder
unlocked your potential to unlock, relock
annex, asseverate? Own? Did he know?

Had he seen boomerangs before? When he threw
you, could he foresee your return as vulture?
His future as carrion? How proud he'd be.

EVERY BOY WHO KILLS IN THE GHETTO IS ME

I am no Richter scale. I know nothing
of earthquakes, but I can explain
how the hand shakes as the trigger
squeeze reaches a pause point.
I could describe how both hands
vibrate the morning after a boy
drops in the wake of their treachery.

I have killed myself, and lived to tell
the story. Is it still suicide if the you
that dies carries a different heart,
answers to another name, grew
on another block? When your dad
says sorry to his in the courtroom, is it
sorry your son died or sorry mine didn't?

CAGED CONCORDE

Protest is the purest honesty. This is what pushes us
forward. This is what cleans the house.

Gregory Porter

Lions are made for cages, she said.
She told me to *be good*. I brushed
my mane to impress a world that
will never hear the lyrics of my song,
only the roar of my vocal. I wear
assumptions to every single party,
but apparently these aren't red
carpet rags. I avoid the cameras
as much as they avoid me, allowing
myself to believe maybe it was me
who started this. I shouldn't be here,
or there, or any of the parties where
my invite is spat through bread knife
teeth. I am no lion. I am Concorde,
destined to slice through stratosphere,
to rise above and stay there. I am
still carrying this cage, but it will not
slow my speed, or crash this plane.

TOMORROW, YESTERDAY, TODAY

1

'Tomorrow,' he said. Somewhere between
raising our hoods and our knuckles separating,
fists pressing love into ghetto goodbyes,
he said tomorrow and meant it.
The difference between broken promises
and miscarried promises is intention.
Green leaves cleaved from trees by young hands,
fallen before fall. Evergreen was not the plan.
How his brothers grow brown and withered
in his absence, hoping only the claws of gravity
will grasp them, lest they be snatched too soon.
The promise of winter provides no comfort;
after witnessing cold bodies in warm climates
we don't ask for winter, only for tomorrow.

2

Flying and crashing. He spoke of death
how you might speak of a grandparent
you don't visit, longing and repentant,
like he would meet her soon, embrace her –
how cold could life be that the warmth
of expiration comes like chequered flags? Celebrated ends,
but podium places are gone, too many
passed before, lost already. Fallen.
There is nothing groundbreaking about graves
for the young. Water off a coffin's top,
when the sky shares your mother's grief and weeps.
If we were seeds, this would be the onset
of life; we are not seeds – descending,
derailing, flying and crashing.

3

Dreaming of life, experiencing nothing,
he felt the morning slide through his hands.
How to capture your own life before it drips
away? When is death more than the outcome
of life? When is this life not cartwheeling towards
extinction? Our desires have been dismembered
before our eyes, backs stabbed by those who told us
to put our knives down. We have trickled into a
world outside ourselves. We are not stuck,
but movement is a myth we were sold
in bad faith. They handed us hope, never saying
it was a tug-of-war rope. We have been clinging.
We dream of life, knowing dreams don't
come true, but they do come consistently.

4

I could cry, turn my back on decay
or smile at death how she smiles
at me. Familiar. We have been
face-to-face so many times that I know
how the corners of her eyes flutter
before her sneer breaks worlds down
to dust. She has blown lives from
the tops of cabinets, watched them
become impossible to see, breathed
them in, exhaled ponderousness
so that it may land on the shoulders
of survivors. The living will always
be buried with the dead, though we
still profess that the opposite is true.

5

A fox lying dead, middle of the road,
feels unavoidable, was unavoidable.
Wasn't avoided; a void is left
where expected death lands, heavy
as emptiness on apathy. Light carries
but cannot lift gloom from this place,
this place where foxes cross roads
that their siblings perished on,
like Black boys, heading to school
or walking to their burial.
Nobody jokes about foxes'
motivation for crossing roads;
we suppose it a necessity,
don't blink when it kills them.

6

Who speaks to the dead, carries them,
cares for them beyond their expiry date?
Who tells the story of people whose value
cannot be measured through conventional
means? They will not mention me in their
history books; why would they? I would not uphold
their legacies; why would they value mine?
There are no secrets here,
no veil for this process. So much of history
is a celebration in the future by those
who paid for the present, for its opulence,
for the walls that kept poverty away,
knowing that its existence here can be
separated from us when the story is told.

7

Like guarantees we don't trust but need.
Like war in the name of peace, not pieces.
Like me if somebody liked me enough to be
like me. Please feels like an archaic word,
like joy in the plasma leaving ventricles,
like home if the heart walked out. Crushed
like boys in ghettos who smile at the pain.
Like stories of abuse told by victims, laughing
like abusers, whose lack of originality cuts
like wind across faces; same wind, but faces
like the weather, changing – whether reigning
like kings and queens and vampires, danger
like love. Love like losers, who hold nothing.
Like waterfalls. Giving and giving and giving.

8

Yesterday, we said today. Well,
we said tomorrow, but we're
here now. We said tomorrow;
I am here now. Now you are
yesterday, like reminiscing,
regret, you are re-e-wind,
but the crowd is silent.
We have failed to earn our
reversal, your reprieve.
We are tideless water, sitting.
You are yesterday, old cards,
birthdays past, lost
pirouetting in the wind
for yesterday.

9

Worn and wearied is a way of existence
round here. Loss has a way of repeating
its cuts, like a saw through wood, teeth
biting deeper each time. When I called
you, and you didn't answer, I left two
voicemails; you were a dickhead in both.
You will never hear those words, but
sometimes, when the shower hides
my tears, I think of how we would have
laughed if you had made it to the morning.
Each stroke of the blade is miniscule,
barely a scratch on the surface at first.
In the end, it will not be a slice that
causes the break, but the constant friction.

10

Look at me. Optimism died with my friends.
It used to climb me like ivy on oak.
I wore it to every function, consistent
if not fashionable, hopeful when not whole.
Jaded by death, wearied by life;
broken, blade blunted by battles I can't win.
I can't breathe. Words from Black men under blue boots,
words from Black womxn under white oppression.
The legs of my pain keep kicking the walls,
the walls of my brain, shock-absorbent now.
Waking and sleeping at wartime. Round here
we practise affliction and disaster.
Despondency is a background colour
on the canvas of existence round here.

11

I carried boxes and bodies and asteroids,
held up the sky while it wept; you never saw
my tears, never felt my thunderous rumble.
Desperate to keep the dry face of masculinity,
skipping like CD players back in the day
when we ran without warning or purpose.
Scratches on CDs are cadavers of music.
How we inspect them for stories, for truth,
how we endeavour to understand loss
when the day is a ball of knuckles in the gut
that repeats, skipping, skipping, skipping.
'Real Gs don't die' is a call to heaven, pleading
for it not to take us back, a cry to each other:
'Don't forget me if I go first, I won't forget you.'

12

Crashing into Earth, reaching through time.
The second hand has been moving faster
than usual, it seems. We smile for the
ghosts who we can't see but who see us
whispering prayers. Faith is a secret;
show it to your god and to your friends
who step with you on snow but leave
no footprints behind. Let the world see
the veneer or the sneer, the elated
or the murderous. If they could witness
how you sob when the pillow won't hug
you back, if they could see how you
practise the last words of your existence,
they may put you on that stage to perform.

13

Trapped in the middle of it all, waiting
for nothing to happen. I've never seen
that before. Silence hasn't visited
my block for as long as I can remember.
The small Michael Scofield in my mind
hasn't said a thing to me in weeks,
but I can hear him talking to someone;
I'm starting to wonder if he is here
to break me out or break out of me.
I don't know what the tattoos mean,
so I wait, confined, solitary. People
gather, transfixed by the juvenile living
inside this adult frame, confused
by the noise and silence and the fight.

14

Today my neck aches. Head hanging
like the washing in the rain.
Today is a JD drawstring bag
after the corner is torn, inevitable.
Today is non-negotiable, it is
every birthday we will celebrate
in your absence, every song
that will simultaneously fill my
heart and decimate my spirit.
I cry, adding to rivers
I can't swim, stuck in a current that
pulls me under. Currently I am fixed
on yesterday, scared of tomorrow.
Today is your absence, my loss.

15

Tomorrow, he said. Somewhere between
flying and crashing, he spoke of death,
dreaming of life, experiencing nothing.
I could cry. Turn my back on decay.
A fox lying dead, middle of the road.
Who speaks to the dead, carries them
like guarantees we don't trust but need?
Yesterday, we said today. Well
worn and wearied is a way of existence;
look at me. Optimism died with my friends;
I carried boxes and bodies and asteroids,
crashing into Earth reaching through time,
trapped in the middle of it all, waiting.
Today my neck aches. Head hanging.

NOTES

The shape of 'Same/Energy' was inspired by Toby Campion's 'Nits'.

'When the Roll Is Called up Yonder' is an adaptation of a monologue from my play *GrimeBoy*.

'Angela David Said More #1' is an erasure poem, taken from: Angela Davis. 'Education and Liberation: Black Women's Perspective'. *Women, Race & Class*. London: Penguin, 2019.

'Angela David Said More #2' is an erasure poem, taken from: Angela Davis. 'Communist Women'. *Women, Race & Class*. London: Penguin, 2019.

'Angela David Said More #3' is an erasure poem, taken from: Angela Davis. 'Rape, Racism and the Myth of the Black Rapist'. *Women, Race & Class*. London: Penguin, 2019.

'Curfew Breakers' is an erasure poem, taken from: Ronan Bergman. *Rise and Kill First*. London: John Murray, 2018.

ACKNOWLEDGEMENTS

Thank you to everyone at Burning Eye, especially Bridget, for facilitating the creation of this book.

Thank you to *Poetry Birmingham Literary Journal*, which was the first home for part of the poetry sequence *Tomorrow, Yesterday, Today*.

Thank you to the poets, facilitators and friends who have seen this work in various forms and helped me to develop it and myself, including my Room 204 cohort, Hannah Swingler, Jane Commane, Anne Holloway, Chris McLoughlin, Jamie Thrasivoulou, Akor Opaluwah and my whole Big White Shed Arvon family.

Thank you, Caleb Femi and Vanessa Kisuule, who looked at this completed work before anyone else and were generous enough to say nice things.

Thank you, Roger Robinson. I sent you the manuscript that I would have submitted for this book, and you told me it wasn't where it needed to be. You were right! But, more than that, you invested time and energy into showing me things that have allowed me to develop not just this book, but also who I am as a writer. I will be forever better, and forever grateful.

Adrian B Earle, my brother, your attention to detail when looking at this manuscript is appreciated more than you know, but, more than that, as a collaborator, as an example and as a friend, you push me to be better.

Dr Charley Barnes, thank you for finding time and energy, at short notice, to give me exactly what I needed from an editor when I sent you an early version of this manuscript. You're a hero, pal.

Kerri, you are everything! You've made my existence possible and purposeful for well over a decade now. It always makes me question your decision making.

Lightning Source UK Ltd.
Milton Keynes UK
UKHW012013270821
389593UK00002B/137